let's play house

stylish living with children

Lannoo

foreword

When you become a parent, you say goodbye to your neat and perfectly styled home. Because, when kids come along, they come with stuff – lots of it. Now you are left with heaps of toys and mess stowed away in corners – chaos that is expertly concealed, or ignored completely, in glossy home decor magazines.

That's why I wanted to take a look inside the homes of young families where toys are a part of the ambience, kids bring energy and joy, and parents don't think twice about sacrificing most of their living space for cleverly styled rooms, colourful play areas and creative storage. Interior design is and has always been a great passion of mine, even after going through a hellish renovation that lasted almost three years. Since the birth of my daughters, I've focused most of my energy on children's rooms and how other parents find a way to integrate kids' stuff into their interior in a playful, creative way.

When I leaf through design magazines, I'm always a bit sad to see how certain things have been moved or hidden for the sake of the 'perfect' shot. High chairs, a commode, toys and cuddly toys are part of the reality of living with children, and can also be quite beautiful.

Another of my pet peeves is that these same magazines often overlook children's rooms, and don't give them the attention they truly deserve. New parents often put huge amounts of energy and effort into decorating their children's bedrooms, and it's a pity that these rooms are left out. I personally feel that our daughters' bedrooms are the funnest spaces in the house. And after making this book I know that plenty of other parents feel the same. I'd like to thank those mums and dads for allowing us into their homes, sharing practical tips and tricks, and recommending their favourite shops.

Hannelore Veelaert also deserves a special mention here, because she photographed all the Belgian houses in this book so beautifully and honestly with the help of her friend Oswald Cromheecke. Also a big thank you to Niels Famaey and Viktoria De Cubber for believing in this project and giving me the freedom to explore my ideas, to Tina Smedts of the Poedelfabriek for her beautiful designs, and to my dearest husband and children for their unwavering support and inspiration.

Finally, I would like to dedicate this book to my father, who unfortunately was unable to see its publication. No one had a greater love of stylish interiors, both with and without children, and it is thanks to my father that I grew up sharing his passion for interiors, design and colour.

Joni

contents

What used to be an office space later became a dining room and now serves as a playroom. Living with children can radically change the layout of your house, as Marieke and David discovered. 'To avoid toys getting scattered throughout the house, we gave the children their own play corner. It's a space where they can play to their heart's content and leave things in a mess, as long as the rest of the house is tidy,' laughs Marieke.

residents
Marieke (student counsellor),
David (business manager of Newdays
graphic agency), daughter Lili (6),
son Marcel (4) and daughter Lea (1)
Zarren, Belgium
Want to see more?
@marieke_deman

**playful
serenity**

Of course, stray toys turn up here and there, and furniture and white walls get grubby faster with children in the house, but Marieke also really likes some of the children's things. 'It brings life into the place, and just having the children around, seeing their creativity, makes it so homely.' What's her secret when it comes to only allowing visually pleasing toys into the home? 'If you go toy shopping in stores that have a great selection, you can give the kids a little push in the right direction. We just try to avoid chain stores that sell a lot of gaudy plastic, glittery stuff and duvets with certain themes.'

Although white is the principal colour in this extensively renovated home, Marieke has recently started to enjoy and use colour. 'If Lili and Marcel had their way, they'd have brighter shades in their bedroom, but I prefer more muted tones. And for now, they're okay with that!'

By using that neutral colour palette throughout the house, this home breathes comfort and serenity. The calmness of these quiet tones even continues into the nursery and play corner. The colour of the walls, the shade of the duvets and even the materials of the (mini) furniture create a beautiful unity.

Budget-friendly spice racks from Ikea also come in handy in the nursery, where they can serve as a bookshelf or, if installed upside down, as a handy clothes hanger to showcase pieces that deserve to be seen.

Many parents consider a changing table in the living room an eyesore but a necessary evil. Marieke came up with a nice alternative by freeing up a spot on a sideboard and installing an Olli Ella care basket there.

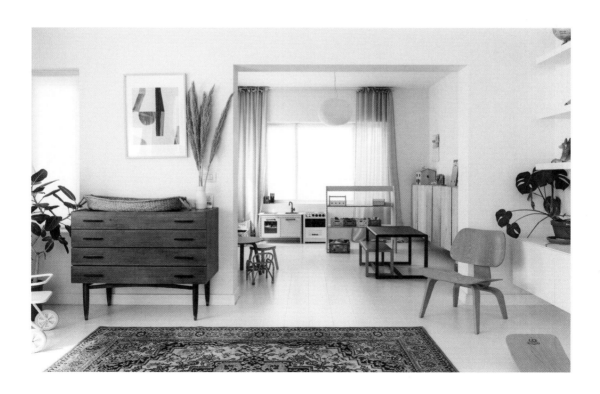

DIY
dream room

Real estate in Stockholm is very pricey, so when Anna and Joncha decided to buy something in their favourite neighbourhood, they could only afford a small one-bedroom apartment. Because their son Sonny Lou was too old to sleep in their room, they placed an extra wall between the kitchen and the living room to create a children's room. Although tiny, the room has everything a child could wish for.

residents
Anna (photographer), Joncha (writer/musician) and son Sonny Lou (8)
Stockholm, Sweden
Want to see more?
@annamalmbergphoto

To make the best use of the available space, Joncha built a custom bed, with plenty of storage space underneath. The raised bed was a space-saving choice, but luckily Sonny Lou thinks it's cool to sleep so high up.

Joncha also designed Sonny Lou's small desk. Crafted from the same material as the bed, it ties the room together beautifully. Now that Joncha has developed a taste for carpentry, he's looking forward to creating more pieces of furniture in the future. They inject character and a unique twist to any interior, especially if space is at a premium.

Anna believes that small spaces can easily feel crowded and cluttered, but she knows how to handle that. 'Too many different colours and toys soon create a sense of chaos and untidiness. So I made a point of choosing neutral shades for the interior. That way, the space feels like a balanced whole, and the space seems larger than it actually is.'

But for Anna it isn't just about aesthetics. Since becoming a mum, sustainability and health have become very important. And when picking out furniture, toys and paint, for example, she always looks for natural alternatives. For walls and furniture, she uses AURO eco-friendly paint and often scours flea markets and thrift stores for fun interior accessories and toys to reduce her carbon footprint.

family house
with history

Caroline felt even more motivated to create an intimate vibe in this Victorian family home to give her growing children lots of wonderful memories. She achieved her vision by indulging in her favourite colours and patterns and by giving a special place to her many holiday souvenirs.

residents
Caroline (founder Apolina Kids),
Martin (graphic designer) and
daughters Veda (6) and Bonnie (5)
East London, UK
Want to see more?
@apolina_kids

'Until we bought it a few years ago, this house – built in the nineteenth century – had been lived in by generations of the same family. The last time the house was renovated was in the 1970s, so there was quite an eclectic colour scheme going on before we started renovating,' laughs Caroline.

Even now the house is a riot of colour, although the young family prefers a soft palette, with the exception of the children's room where a vivid wallpaper by Svenskt Tenn steals the show. 'We deliberately opted for more colour in the girls' room because it had to be a bright, playful space. This room also spotlights our love of crafts and fabrics as a way of encouraging our daughters to explore their creativity,' says Caroline.

'Because the house was designed around the children, you'll find them playing everywhere.' Caroline: 'The children often play in the living room, as well as in the garden or in their bedroom, or even in my studio, where they like to tinker with empty boxes or fabric remnants. We often gather at the table to make craft projects or draw together, as you can see from the stains and scratches on its surface. But the girls love bath times most of all – that's when their imaginations run wild, and they can't stop laughing!'

Although the sofa and dining table are a little the worse for wear, Caroline and Martin won't buy replacements until the children are a little more careful. There's nothing that a stylish tablecloth or a decorative throw and a bit of love can't camouflage for a couple of years...

residents
Charlotte (founder studio.mijmer),
Tom (port engineer) and Julius (1)
Antwerp, Belgium
Want to see more?
@charlottegoorden

a messy house is a happy house

'Your home doesn't have to become an indoor playground because you have children. Naturally, there'll be garish toys all over about the place, but you can stash them out of sight in cool crates and baskets,' say Charlotte and Tom. Their interiors have hardly changed since their son, Julius, was born. 'Things are bound to get broken now and then. Putting a new vase on the side table may not be the best idea, but I'll probably keep doing it.'

Charlotte was thrilled at the thought of creating a nursery. 'Decorating an empty, white room from scratch, I just couldn't wait!' Although she had no mood board or theme for the nursery, she was sure of one thing. On social media, she had seen a photo of an old sturdy cabinet that had been restored and painted. It was just what she wanted! While heavily pregnant, she visited different thrift shops every week, but found nothing. By the time Julius was born, he still had no wardrobe...
A few months later Charlotte made one last try, and this time stumbled upon an ugly musty-smelling brown cupboard. 'My husband went crazy, but I was overjoyed. First, I painted the wardrobe white, then green, blue, apple-blue-sea-green, but the only shade I fell in love with was this blue-grey hue. The sound of the doors squeaking when they open still puts a smile on my face!'

When choosing the shades for the rest of the room, Charlotte was inspired by the soft, warm tones that she finds most appealing, such as blue, dark yellow, grey and green. She wanted to avoid something that was too boyish or cliché.

According to Charlotte, a children's room should be a place where they can be inspired and fantasise, so posters, flags, bookshelves and playful details are essential. 'Let your child make up stories about the octopus on his cupboard and the fish on the wall.' She believes in staying true to her own style and not just copying from others.

At home, Julius is most often found in the kitchen. 'The cat is usually there,' explains Charlotte, 'and it draws him like a magnet. Plus there's lots to discover: cupboards and drawers that open, chairs that can be moved and the large window with a view of the garden.'

Although their son brings a lot of fun into the house, the constant mess took some getting used to. 'It never ends. I can give the house a good clean and ten minutes later it's full of potting soil, toys, clothes, nappies... That irritated me in the beginning, but now it doesn't bother me, and I actually find it charming. When we find toy cars in our shoes or a spoon with the chickens, we just laugh!' says Charlotte.

residents
Constance (pop-up event planner),
Dorian (contractor), daughter
Jouan (7) and son Joseph (3)
Basque Country, France

When Constance and Dorian bought this house, they were more in love with the location than the somewhat run-down property. Their purchase was the start of an eight-year renovation project, with Dorian doing everything himself, aided by his father and brother, both skilled handymen. Only three original walls could be preserved, but now the couple has the house of their dreams: a white bungalow near the sea with a separate wing for the children.

year-round holiday home

When renovations began, the couple had no children, so tackled the open concept kitchen and living space, the office area, and the master bedroom first. In the final phase, they turned an outbuilding into a new wing, where the children now have free rein. The annex is ingeniously connected to the original building by a glass corridor. At the end of that glass corridor, Jouan and Joseph share a large bedroom and have their own bathroom consisting of a half wall topped by beautiful sections of glass.

'As a child, I always dreamed of sharing a room with my sister. That's why I wanted one large bedroom for my children. Once they reach their teens and need more privacy, the room can easily be divided. Their bathroom was designed with this in mind, and has an access door on two sides,' explains Constance. 'The children's bedroom also has sliding doors that open onto the patio, so they can easily take all their toys outside. It's such a joy to watch them playing there!'

The home, with its holiday vibes, is dominated by white and soft pastel colours. The furnishings are a fusion of DIY projects, vintage finds and heirlooms from family and friends. Constance: 'When I was little, my father often woke me up early at weekends to accompany him on jaunts to flea markets looking for treasures. I still do it. You can find the most amazing things for the least amount of money.'

These second-hand treasures also feature prominently in the nursery. Although the real eye-catcher is Jouan's custom-made bed with handy storage space. Some of Constance's grandmother's old wardrobes were also given a new coat of paint and a new lease of life in this playful space. They create a warm atmosphere that's impossible to create with new furniture.

party
of five

How do you take a practical approach to co-parenting when you live with five children? Anne and her ex-partner Filip found the solution, 'bird nesting', in which the kids live in the family space, and the parents rotate every week. That way, everyone gets to enjoy this imaginative home.

<u>**residents**</u>
Anne (co-manager Maison Slash),
Kato (15), Lola (13), Lukas and
Ella (twins, 12) and Fee (9)
Vilvoorde, Belgium
Want to see more?
@mamavanvijf

Finding a large enough house started with a search for the right number of bedrooms. Anne: 'This house has five bedrooms, so in theory there aren't enough for everyone to have their own space, although that's not been a big problem so far. The twins are sharing a room at the moment, but Lola and Kato also slept in the same room for a while. It depends a little on who needs a bit of extra privacy at the time.'

The children don't spend a lot of time in their rooms; they prefer to hang out in the living room or at the kitchen table and enjoy playing games together on the mezzanine. The children play throughout the house, which does have an impact. 'I don't think the ground floor of our house would have looked any different if I hadn't had children, or had a smaller family, but it would have been a little easier. With five kids, the place soon gets dirty and things get broken all the time. If you look, you'll see hand prints on a lot of the walls, and marks on the white floors.'

One room that they would have designed differently if they'd had a smaller family is the bathroom. It now has no fewer than three sinks, and two adjacent showers have been installed. 'Much more practical than a bath. It's like what you often see at indoor swimming pools,' Anne explains.

Anne loves interiors that are open. As you can see in the custom-made kitchen with its open cabinets, and in the XL version of the String shelving system, which is a real eye-catcher in the dining room. It is home to all of the books, with a sprinkling of thrift shop treasures, travel souvenirs and the kids' craft projects.

'What's the use of having things if you hide them behind doors? I think it's far better to see everything on the shelves, even if it is sometimes a bit of a mess. But someone who only has beautiful things can only make a beautiful mess,' laughs Anne. 'I wouldn't be able to live in a clean, styled home. The apartment where I live alone every other week looks almost the same. Only I have a few more plants there.'

tranquil but
colourful

If it were up to Rio and Otis, their bedrooms would have looked a little different – read: much more colourful - but their mum, Janniche, prefers a tranquil mood and restful shades. She says it's important that the house has a unified feel to create a homey, relaxing vibe. That's why she wanted the children's rooms to blend in with the rest of the house rather than stand out too much.

residents
Janniche (UX designer and
freelance interior stylist),
Johan (photographer),
daughter Rio (8) and son Otis (5)
Stockholm, Sweden
Want to see more?
@bloggaibagis

This doesn't mean that the rooms in this Scandinavian home are plain and dull, quite the contrary. Janniche is very aware of her children's tastes, but prefers to use a toned-down version or pastel variant of their favourite colours. 'I don't think kids' walls should necessarily be painted in their favourite colour. You can add their favourite shades as accent colours in details and accessories: a fun duvet cover, a rug, curtains or small furniture items,' she explains.

Another way to create a sense of calm in the home, especially with young children, is to provide sufficient storage space. She had large built-in wardrobes installed in the children's room to store all the toys out of sight. The children have easy access to their things, and tidying up never takes too long.

Janniche works as a freelance interior stylist and enjoys making and building things herself. She's a whiz at designing snug sitting areas or creating a handy desk space. She also has a talent for wallpapering, painting and DIY. That's why her interior is never the same for long. Yet is always tranquil, stylish and cohesive.

You don't have to hide away every toy. Why not highlight the most interesting playthings by putting them in a display case. It's a great way to add a decorative touch to a room without the objects gathering dust. And you can make subtle changes to the decor by putting other toys or accessories in the spotlight.

vintage girls' house

Lupa and Luz live with their mum, Dorith, and have christened their home the 'girls' house'. And, as you might expect, the girls' house is a homage to one particular shade – yes, you've guessed it – pink. It's also crammed with vintage and unique second-hand gems; you won't find many new items here.

residents
Dorith (architect) and
daughters Lupa (8) and Luz (6)
Antwerp Belgium

Dorith: 'For me, buying vintage is a form of sustainable consumption. I like to recycle and restore things that others throw in the skip. I occasionally buy contemporary items that I like, but always make sure that they're extremely well made. The sixties furniture in our house has proven its durability over the years. It would be nice if my daughters could enjoy the new things that we add today in 50 years' time.'

A yellow children's bed and a blue children's bed, a mint-green wardrobe and a tricolour Tomado racks adorn the children's room, but a myriad different colours can also be found in the rest of the house. Yet everything breathes harmony and unity. Dorith's secret? 'Choosing colours is a slow process for me, but I always end up somewhere in Le Corbusier's polychromy.'

Like the choice of colours, the placement of the items is often the result of an informed decision. Dorith: 'Sometimes it takes me a year to find the ideal place for a coat rack or a flower pot. Children are the perfect excuse to turn my house into even more of a cabinet of curiosities. I like to surround myself and my daughters with unusual things. You'll find mini still lifes of objects, next to or against a background of books, photos or record sleeves dotted all over the house. For example, our sunglasses stand on wooden noses in front of a record sleeve featuring Elvis Costello's glasses.'

For Lupa and Luz, this house full of vintage treasures is the ideal place to let their imaginations run wild. Dorith often comes across amazing tableaux her daughters have made from their toys. 'I recently found an entire Playmobil adventure playground hidden among the leaves of a large houseplant. They really use whatever they find. I lost a slipper and found it being used as a doll's sleeping bag. The girls build Kapla houses combined with sections from a marble roller coaster, polystyrene foam and bubble wrap where blended families of bears, Barbie dolls and Lego figures live. Everything gets mixed up. Amazing!' laughs Dorith. 'But cleaning up all these tableaux when the cleaning lady comes isn't as much fun!'

Dorith allows the children to play with everything, which makes for a relaxed, fun vibe. 'I have a lot of valuable design pieces at home,' says Dorith, 'but I've never spent a lot of money on them. Well-designed furnishings are pretty robust. To me, an expensive couch that shouldn't get dirty is a poorly designed couch,' she says.

After a year of house hunting, Emma and Liam knew they would have to act quickly as soon as they found a home that they liked. This airy, bright house with a double-fronted window was a godsend, and after just one visit, they decided to buy. When Emma was just four months pregnant, they were able to move into their very first family home.

residents
Residents: Emma (blogger),
Liam (composer), son Finn (7)
and daughter Violet (4)
London, UK
Want to see more?
@finlay_fox

an explosion of colour and art

During the renovation, Emma discovered that furnishing a children's room can be deeply satisfying. 'There's something liberating about creating a childlike space – you can really indulge your love of colour and playful details. As I went along, I felt more confident about experimenting with colour, and dared to let colours pop!' she says. And this confidence shows because the children's rooms are a joy to the eye. The rest of the house also bursts with creativity and playful details.

'A family home often grows with its residents. The interior always changes, especially when you have young children. Because of its practical location on the ground floor and proximity to the kitchen, it wasn't long before my office was converted into a playroom. That way we can keep an eye on them when we are cooking or when visitors come over,' Emma explains. But having the children playing in the vicinity of the parents also means their toys and playthings are always in sight. 'When it comes to toy buying, we've been able to avoid plastic. In principle, all of the children's toys match the interior of the house. Of course, there are always toys all over the place, but that stopped bothering me a long time ago. As long as they're all stored away by the end of the day.'

The walls of the house are graced by beautiful and unique artworks. The eye-catcher in the dining room is the apple print *Uno, La Mela* by Enzo Mari from 1963. In the playroom and living room there is a blend of personal photos, oil paintings by Emma's grandfather, drawings of the children and modern artwork. Emma likes an eclectic whole that gives a home personality. 'The objects we hang on the wall are constantly changing. I love to mix up different sizes and styles. It also gives the children an incentive to be creative when they see their artwork hanging on the wall.'

For the children's rooms, Emma found inspiration in Pippi Longstocking and Wes Anderson. The result is playful and colourful spaces that are exclusively decorated by vintage and second-hand furniture collected over the years by this creative climate activist.

residents
Emma (journalist / writer / climate activist), John (bio-informatics specialist) and daughters Majken (5) and Bodil (4)
Stockholm, Sweden
Want to see more?
@emmasundh

'I've always been very chaotic and untidy, so I can't really blame the kids for the apartment being a mess 99 per cent of the time,' admits Emma honestly. In that sense, becoming a mum didn't change very much, although it had a big impact on her attitudes to travel, interior design and fashion.

'I worked as a journalist for various fashion magazines and, like everyone else, was a frequent flyer. But I began to regard the reports on climate change in a different light and started wondering: What will I say if, later on, my kids ask me what I did to save the planet while I had the chance? I wanted to answer that I'd done my bit, and not come up with feeble excuses. So I chose to live differently.'

She is already raising her children in this sustainable way of life. 'For example, we only buy pre-loved clothing, all toys and interior items are second-hand, we eat local food and rarely throw anything away. Majken and Bodil are also used to taking the bike to the supermarket and travelling by train instead of by plane,' says Emma.

Her sustainable lifestyle hasn't dulled her style – Emma's interior is colourful, cheerful and, above all, 100 per cent unique.

For fun second-hand or vintage items, you don't have to comb flea markets or auction sites. You can also easily borrow items from friends or family to reduce your carbon footprint. Isn't it great to see your own children sleeping in a cot or bed you once slept in?

playing
together
under
the eaves

residents
Fien (marketing manager),
Anthony (self-employed),
daughters Liv (5) and Cilou (2)
Antwerp, Belgium
Want to see more?
@fiendq

In a country like Belgium where it rains regularly, you need a house with a variety of nooks and crannies where your children can play. Anthony and Fien transformed the attic space of their house into a play area and bedroom after the birth of their first daughter. And now that she has a sister, it gets even more use.

'When you have to play indoors all day because it's raining outside, it's great for the girls to be able to play on a different floor. And I really enjoy spending time in our converted loft space, in both children's rooms, actually. Particularly when they're nice and tidy. You can tell that a lot of attention went into designing the children's rooms. It's much more interesting than our bedroom, I think,' laughs Fien.

'There are so many fantastic interior accessories for kids. I love all of that, and that's why the children's rooms never look the same for long. I often buy new things and then discard something else or move things from one nursery to another. I like such an eclectic feel and an interesting combination of old and new stuff. Liv is also starting to show more and more interest in it. She chose the OYOY 'Follow the Rainbow' wall rug herself.

Although the young family enjoys living in their 1930s home, Fien and Anthony are looking for a new house. Fien: 'The children are growing up and we need more space. If we move to a bigger house I'd be able to keep all our belongings. They have sentimental value for me, and will make a new place feel homey. So when we go on house viewings, I always take a good look around to see if there's space for everything.'

For the time being, the Ikea Stuva benches and the countless storage boxes and crates offer a solution. Fien says these storage bins are essential. 'I prefer to sort the toys by type in different stacking bins. One for the puzzles another for the dolls, and yet another for the animals and so on. Liv and Cilou tend to be drawn to the box at the top, so I can easily make subtle changes and vary what they play with. And they're super handy for tidying up, which is of course a big plus.'

residents
Irene (founder Atelier Sukha), Gabriel
(consultant) and daughter Juul (2)
Amsterdam, The Netherlands
Want to see more?
@ateliersukha of sukha.nl

from dark garage to light, open-plan house

Wherever Irene and Gabriel are in the house, they can keep an eye on their daughter, Juul. That's the big advantage of this open-plan house where the few walls consist of a mix of old windows. And being able to see the canal in front of the house, and the trees in the garden from anywhere inside the space, is a fantastic bonus.

Although the house is very open and transparent, it also offers space for everyone to spend time alone when they need to. In the wooden tepee that is filled with pillows or in the bedroom, there is room to read, sleep or meditate in peace. The bathroom is also an enclosed space, but is intentionally placed next to the kitchen to be close to the living space. Irene: 'When Juul is in the bath, I can cook dinner and still keep an eye on her.'

To transform the dark 300-square-metre garage into its present state, the roof was completely demolished and new windows, including some skylights, were installed. The couple were delighted to discover exposed wooden beams, which were renovated and replaced where necessary.

'Afterwards the floors and walls were covered with clay. That has a cooling effect in the summer and creates warmth in the winter,' explains Irene. 'Moreover, you also have very beautiful colours that fit perfectly with our interior. We chose a green-white shade and added some colour accents for Juul, such as the red sofa and a blue chair. She really loves our house. She can just cycle inside, has her own wooden playhouse and a tepee where she can read books by herself.'

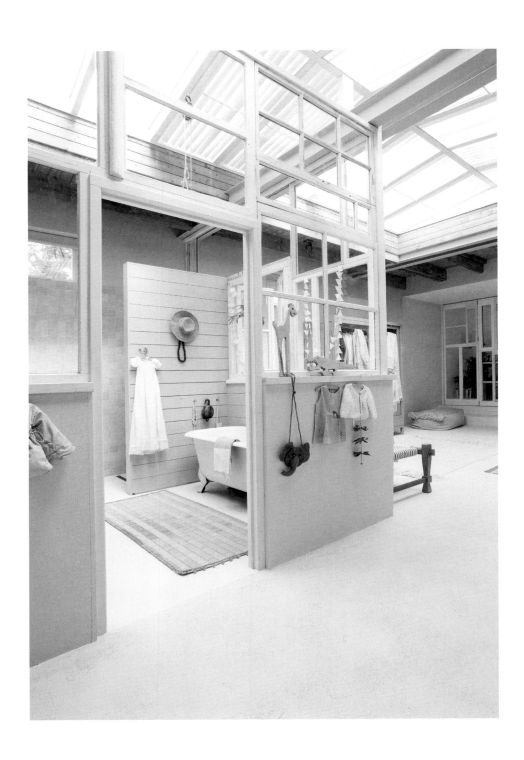

house
of cubs

As a stay-at-home mum, Isabel naturally spends most of her time at home with the children. So she wanted to create a cosy home that everyone enjoys spending time in, where they can sleep soundly, play to their heart's content, and tidy everything away quickly afterwards.

residents
Isabel (stay-at-home mother),
Stephen (maintenance planner)
and sons Christian (3)
and Ethan (18 months)
Perth, Australia
Want to see more?
@house.of.cubs

Isabel: 'Since becoming parents, my husband and I have discarded or stored a lot of less child-friendly things, and added plenty of things for the boys. We may have decluttered some of our belongings, but an abundance of new toys and possessions have taken their place, and it makes the kids' rooms cosy.'

Despite the clutter, Isabel has created a unified, inviting interior. She describes her decorating style as 'vintage Scandinavian meets boho' with a deep love of rattan and natural brown tones. The same colour palette is found in the children's rooms and playrooms, with an understated animal theme for an extra playful touch.

Because a nursery needs to combine cheerfulness with practicality for the parents, Isabel finds it easier to furnish nurseries than toddlers' rooms. 'When your child is a little older, you really need to find out what they like, something that sparks their imagination and that you can get excited about, too.' In the playroom, it's all about the play area and storage space. With an XXL play mat, a handy wardrobe system from Ikea and the hand-made labels from the Australian brand Zane's Room, she turned it into a room that's snug yet practical.

With three young children, the house is often a little crowded. That is why Katrien and Olivier are happy to have the extra outdoor space at their recently renovated 'Villa Verde'. When Thelma, Malo and Richard are outside swimming, feeding birds or go-karting among the trees, Katrien can enjoy a moment's quiet inside...

residents
Katrien (ceramist), Olivier (doctor), Thelma (10), Malo (7) and Richard (5)
Flemish Brabant, Belgium
Want to see more?
@___katrien___ en @atelier_ukiyo

contemporary
sixties vibes

Katrien: 'I am quite a quiet type myself and I have three very lively children, so that can be tough at times! Especially because my husband often has to work long hours and there's only me to keep them in check. But it's great having the house full of their energy. It's a fun kind of chaos, and I love their rich imaginations.'

For Katrien, having children also means taking a more practical approach to the decor, creating little nooks and snug corners so that everyone has their own space, and investing in baskets and storage furniture to collect all the 'stray' toys. A playroom with a television was created for the children where they can spend time alone during the day, or play when the weather's bad.

'I'm also extra careful about materials now – I pick things that can stand up to a bit of wear and tear.

That's why we have a seat with a washable cover and a patio table in our dining room. The kids can paint and mess about on it, and the stains come off easily,' she says. 'The custom cabinets in the hallway are also scratch-resistant and washable. That's an absolute must!'

But aesthetics are important as well. Katrien always chooses attractive items, also for the children. As you can see in the children's rooms, which have been furnished with loving attention and an eye for detail. Sustainability is a consideration here, too. Katrien: 'We consciously choose things that can be given a new lease of life once the children have outgrown them. It's something I look for in clothing, toys and furniture. That's is why I often sell items when the kids have outgrown them. And I just love change, too.'

residents
Laura (architect/contractor), Pieter,
daughter Emilia (7) and son Julius (5)
Overijse, Belgium
Want to see more?
@laumpaum & laum-paum.be

extraordinary living

As an architect and contractor, Laura renovates only old character properties; she never builds new houses. So it made complete sense that the home she would choose for her family would also be an exceptional building. But this renovated former laundry designed by Belgian architect Maxime Brunfaut is beyond extraordinary.

When Laura and Pieter came across this property on the Belgian property website Immoweb, it had been neglected for 30 years and was extremely run-down. Everything was broken and there was talk of concrete rot, but the spaces appealed to them so much that they made an offer anyway. The metamorphosis from a decrepit industrial laundry to a stylish family home took a huge amount of work, but after a few years the family was able to move in.

Laura: 'Because I fell pregnant shortly after the purchase, we chose to renovate the entire house in a child-friendly way. We probably wouldn't otherwise have added the parachute cord suspension lines in the living room, but now I think it adds value. It's a personal touch that you won't see anywhere else, and I'm a big fan of linear aspects anyway.

Our interior is very open, and that's a huge bonus with a family of growing children. The large windows mean that we can see and hear them even when they're alone in their room. Of course, this isn't something they'll be keen on when they reach 16, but time will tell. And we'll find a way around it.

'The children's rooms were decorated in more or less the same way, but there is a clear difference and both have their own colour palette: mint green for Emilia and yellow for Julius, with a special paint effect on the ceiling that extends onto the wardrobe in both rooms. 'It was a spur-of-the-moment thing,' Laura explains. 'I really like continuous lines and patterns, so I thought: why not try? Now that Emilia is getting older, she is starting to ask for shades of pink and is developing her own style, but Julius still thinks it's all fantastic.'

A cosy play corner has been set up under the stairs that connect the landing with the living room, as well as a super-fun swing from Done by Deer. The cupboards in the living room are also packed with toys. Laura: 'I don't have 20 sets of flatware or anything. The mid-century sideboard that holds our record player contains only toys and craft supplies. There's no rule that says toys should be stashed in kiddie-style wardrobes or bins, so why not keep them in a beautifully designed dresser? The children love playing here, but they've also learned that they have to tidy up after themselves every day.'

Two floors and four walls. That was pretty much all you could say about the shell apartment that Laura and Nicolas bought. And it was exactly what architect Laura wanted: an empty space in which she could create a bespoke interior for a growing family.

better
together

residents
Laura (architect), Nicolas (teacher),
daughter Olivia (4) and son Léo (1)
Brussels, Belgium
Want to see more?
lfr_lfr

The ground floor has no interior walls – a deliberate choice so that all the spaces are connected. This makes for a pleasant, spacious living area but also means that, if Olivia and Léo are left to do what they like, the living room and kitchen often look more like a huge playroom. The children love playing in the same room where their parents happen to be.

Laura: 'If we ever move, I'd definitely create a large playroom where they can leave their toys lying around and not have to tidy everything away every night. When we bought the apartment, we didn't have children and I was under the illusion that I'd be able to choose which toys and games came through the door. And I thought I'd be able to keep the amount of stuff in check. We know better now! We've already had to sacrifice several cabinets in the living room to make way for puzzles, board games and craft materials.'

Upstairs, the children share a spacious 45-square-metre bedroom. This allows for a big play area but, with a few stylistic tweaks, each child has their own space and a snug cocoon for sleeping.

The base of the room is a timber floor and white walls, with coloured panelling on one side, and on the other wallpaper with a print. Olivia's side has a rattan bed and a white wardrobe, while Léo has a white bed and a wooden wardrobe. This creates a harmonious style but with lots of contrasts for a playful touch.

When the children are older and need more privacy, the room will be divided in half. Laura knows exactly how she'll do it: by building a low separating wall in the centre, topped by a large glass panel to optimise the light. The room already has two separate access doors. But before that happens, she is looking forward to the bunk bed phase. She also has plans for that, too.

Laura loves DIY as a wonderful way to give the whole house a little more personality. Garlands, pillows, blankets... she's always busy with a craft project. The name garlands and the eucalyptus wreath in the nursery are just some of Laura's fun home-made projects.

According to former interior stylist Margaux, a comfortable bed is the only truly essential element in a children's room, but it would be a shame to leave it at that when there are so many beautiful children's items available. Fortunately, she has two daughters for whom she could furnish a dream room. And we haven't even got to the playroom yet!

residents
Margaux (influencer / content creator), Lucas (estate agent), daughters Ambre (3) and Lison (3 months)
Victoria, Australia
Want to see more?
@thefrenchfolk of thefrenchfolk.com

**of rattan and
rainbows**

'The way you decorate a room can determine whether or not your kids want to play in it. Ambre is busy for hours with her play kitchen, shop and make-up table,' says Margaux. As her daughter got older, she saw the amount of playthings and toys steadily increase: from a small play corner in the living room to a full-fledged playroom full of rattan mini-furniture.

Because she is forever picking up new and exciting ideas, Margaux changes her interior every so often. This ranges from a new cot to re-wallpapering a room or pimping a play kitchen. 'I like to "hack" stuff. It's so much more fun to give things a personal touch. I'd love to transform the Ikea kitchen in a hundred new ways.'

Margaux stripped almost every plastic accessory, with the exception of the tap, from this toy kitchen. She replaced the Perspex in the cabinet doors with cane webbing, the handles with a sleek metal version, and the white cupboards were sanded and then painted in a beautiful rust colour.

A striking feature of this Australian home is the use of wood and rattan, materials that Margaux feels are indispensable in a home space. 'Rattan just goes with everything, you can combine it with vintage pieces or you can place it in a modern interior without any problems – it always works. I also think it makes your interior more homely. Wood always gives a snug, warm feel to an interior. I will always prefer natural materials over plastic or metal.'

Another recurring element in the children's rooms is the use of vintage-looking rainbows, a colour palette that Margaux is in love with. 'The current rainbow trend has something minimalist about it, which means that it fits in almost any room and is much easier to combine than, for example, a floral print,' she concludes.

XXL
playhouse

After seeing the estate agent hammering the 'for sale' signs into the ground, Isabelle immediately called to make an appointment. She and her husband often passed this large detached house and they were always sorry to see it empty. Just pregnant with their second daughter, the couple were looking for a quieter house, especially one with a larger garden. And one thing soon led to another...

residents
Isabelle (secondary school teacher),
Vic (supervisor on chemical production
site), Coco (4), Winnie (2) and
a third daughter on the way
Bevel, Belgium

In just six months, the entire house was gutted and rebuilt. The interior was designed to provide sufficient play space on the ground floor. Both in the reading corner and the television room, there is ample space for the children to play without getting under their parents' feet. The house itself is very child-friendly, with the exception of the pellet stove and some sharp corners in the kitchen, but Isabelle and Vic have taught their children to be careful.

It wasn't long before the walk-in wardrobe was turned into a playroom, with vintage gymnastics mats, cosy cushions, cuddly toys and a pink Playmobil playhouse. Because all the clothes are cleverly – and almost invisibly – stored in built-in wardrobes, there's lots of space for extra toys that can't be stored downstairs.

The house has an individual, eclectic vibe, with a mix of second-hand furniture, bespoke items and Ikea furnishings. 'We never had a particular style or colour theme in mind. Anything goes!' says Isabelle. 'The interior of the nursery is just like the rest of our house. Full of toys and fun, colourful stuff, and the nursery's certainly no different.'

In a toy-filled house, you need plenty of storage space. But, as you can see in this house, you can also use toys and books as decorative objects to give your house extra personality: by arranging your books according to colour and featuring the most beautiful picture books on a wall rack; or getting some cool wardrobes or storage baskets and boxes, such as these colourful folding crates by Aykasa that are used throughout the house.

The couple opted to paint the entire house white and added pops of colour that they can change whenever they like. 'This way, almost every object matches our interior, and we can easily adapt it to meet our needs – which can change quickly. We did the same thing even before we had children, filling the house with bright, playful objects. We particularly like the wooden monkey by Kaj Bojesen that hangs from the wardrobe and the Ferm Living seahorse that decorates the wall. We hope our children like them, too.'

residents
Natacha, Charles and their daughters
Lily (3) and Mila (1.5)
Bordeaux, France

With a black kitchen, a striking deep-green botanical wallpaper in the dining room and white children's rooms with pastel-coloured accents, the interior of this townhouse with its lush green garden is varied to say the least. This is thanks to Natacha, who browses home interior magazines and blogs, and always comes up with fresh ideas.

townhouse bursting with variety

Natacha: 'Sometimes I call Charles at work to tell him that I've rearranged the interior again and to expect a few changes when he comes home.' This young mother has a soft spot for interior design, and a particular penchant for all things bohemian or with a touch of rustic charm. She has a field day at the biannual Bordeaux Quinconces market. 'From now on I really have to keep myself in check, because we've only lived in the house for a year and it is already bursting at the seams,' she laughs.

Initially, the couple wanted a completely white house with a light, pure look, but new elements were soon added. 'When Natacha asked me to buy black paint for the kitchen, I was a bit worried, but now I'm really happy with the result,' says Charles. The other rooms haven't remained exclusively white, either.

Lily's bedroom is an oasis of white with a dash of pastel-coloured accessories and wooden bird nests. A special little highlight here is the desk corner, where dark chalkboard paint was used. A similar bold touch can also be found in Mila's room: she has a peach-coloured accent wall that, with the addition of paper 'pompoms' and rustic rattan furniture, creates a fairy-like atmosphere.

The house originally featured a fourth bedroom that was sacrificed to accommodate a spacious family bathroom. Natacha: 'I am very happy with the result, we spend a lot of time together here. When Charles and I have to get ready in the morning, the girls just play next to us, and when they are in the bath I can sit with them quietly with a magazine in the chair next to them.'

ever-changing

Not a week goes by without Aylin changing something in her decor. Sometimes she moves furniture from one room to another, or relocates smaller accessories temporarily. Daughter Evy's room never looks the same for long either – though this is often down to Evy herself, who likes to litter the whole room with toys.

residents
Aylin, Jeffrey and daughter Evy (4)
Haarlem, The Netherlands
Want to see more?
@okermint

Decorating the nursery was quite a challenge for Aylin. She wanted her daughter to have the biggest bedroom, but then had to find ways to make it cheery and snug. She took it step by step, beginning with the base, a gorgeous shade for the walls paired with a striking wallpaper. Next she added a large hanging lamp, playful rugs, a Manowoods bed and a unique Kroost Vintage wardrobe for the finishing touch.

Evy often says how much she loves her room, and when visitors come over, she always takes them upstairs to show them every corner of her room and all the amazing things there. Her room is often messy, but that's how it should be, says Aylin.

If you have a large nursery or lots of space in your living room, experiment with putting your playset in the centre of the room, rather than in a corner. It's a great way to bring life into the space, and also gives your child plenty of freedom to move (and makes him or her less inclined to draw on the walls).

When your son or daughter has outgrown the cot, you can always store it, pass it on or resell it, but you could think about transforming it into a fun sofa by opening it on one side and filling it with a pile of soft pillows.

Adding a pop of colour to a children's room always brings a bit of fun. When choosing a shade, think about how certain hues will affect your child's mood. Green is perfect in the bedroom because it provides harmony and tranquillity – exactly the atmosphere you want to evoke there.

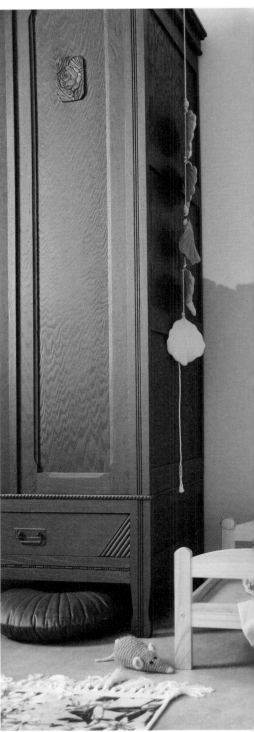

Expect nothing less than stunning decor from an artistic family living in a listed art nouveau building. Like all the other magnificently proportioned rooms in this beautiful house, the children's rooms and the spacious (play) attic were decorated with meticulous care and a dash of grandeur.

residents
Sandrine (artist), Hervé (entrepreneur), son Paul (7) and daughter Fleur (5)
Mulhouse, France

a nod to
art nouveau

Paul and Fleur spend most of their time playing, reading or dancing in the communal areas of the house, but they can retreat to their own personal universe whenever they like. Both children have large bedrooms gorgeously decorated by creative super-talent Sandrine.

Sandrine: 'Now that my children have reached an age where they can communicate their personal likes, I think it's important to reflect their tastes when decorating their rooms. Naturally, I'll always give the decor my own twist and am unconsciously influenced by current interior trends, although I don't follow them slavishly.

'In both children's rooms, I wanted to create a decorative environment that isn't too heavily themed or focused on a particular hobby. When your children are five and seven, their interests change almost by the day... These interiors will grow with them, without us having to change everything all the time.'

In the children's spacious rooms where the art nouveau style is still a clear presence, walls, ceilings, floors and even the built-in wardrobes were entirely painted white. But that is where the similarities between the two rooms end. By using lush colour accents – pink for Fleur and yellow and blue for Paul – each space has its own personality, without being too cliché. To create a cosy sleeping area in the large bedrooms, both children were given a custom-made bed with side walls and a 'roof'. Now they have a comfy, quiet place where they can snuggle down in their own hideaway bed.

Why choose an everyday accent wall when you can create even more impact with an area of colour that flows from the ceiling to the walls and floor, thought Sandrine when finishing Paul's room. It transforms the entire space and creates an unexpected wow effect when you enter.

Black can be playful, too. As you can see from the spacious hall with indoor swing and child-friendly design dog. And in the adjoining television room, adding decorative black polka dots brings a touch of whimsy. And that's not just for kids!

Because the children's room is only separated from the living room by a sliding door, the residents of this small flat tried to create a sense of unity between the two spaces. That's also why there are no loud 'children's colours', and why Ezra's bedroom is a soothing dark aqua green, which perfectly ties in with his current 'sea world theme'.

residents
Sladjana, Haris (managers of the Kitanovic Gallery) and son Ezra (4)
Amsterdam, The Netherlands
Want to see more?
@ezi_mezi

**dark but
bright**

'Ezra wasn't even a year old when, during his first visit to the aquarium, he became enchanted by the underwater world. And he still loves it, as you can see. His room is full of fish, sharks, octopuses. That's what inspired me to pick Annette Weelink's Ocean wallpaper. We listen to what Ezra wants, and decide the decor together as long as I can translate it to our taste. That way, everybody's happy,' says Sladjana.

The orientation and design of the nursery may be a little unusual, but in retrospect Sladjana is very happy with it. 'In the morning we open the sliding doors, and Ezra has one big space to play in. Isn't that great? And although the style of his room blends in nicely with the rest of the home, if we need a little more minimalism, we just close the doors and all the toys are gone,' she explains.

Ezra's room has a clear layout with a reading area, sleeping area, play area and dressing area. It is small, but there is always a kind of order. After a day of playing, everything is cleared away in no time. Most items are stored in a large vintage chest that Ezra calls 'the treasure chest', and the rest of the toys are quickly stashed in handy storage bags.

The many windows of the small apartment let in a sea of daylight, so the home never feels stuffy. But since Ezra's arrival, Sladjana has had to make concessions. 'To me, even a remote control on the table looks untidy. That's why we started to declutter. Now, we have only what we really need. For Ezra, of course, that's slightly different, but I also think it's important that he doesn't get bored and there are enough things to challenge and interest him in our small home.'

a holiday mood

residents
Tessa (stay-at-home mum), Menno (baker) and their three sons, Mees (11), Polle (8) and Guus (5)
Alphen aan den Rijn, The Netherlands
Want to see more?
@tessahop

Inspired by a summer vacation in a French timber holiday cottage, Tessa and Menno decided to build a house in western red cedar on a deserted piece of land just outside Alpen aan den Rijn. The result? A sprawling energy-neutral house with an open-plan living area and lots of space for playing children.

Tessa: 'I want my home to feel calm. I like it when my house is neat and clean. That's why I never leave until everything has been tidied up and put away. When we get back home, we can make a mess again. I really love to see the children playing in the house, but before we go out I make everything's been tidied away. That's why I love all the built-in wooden wardrobes in our house. The whole place is toy-free in next to no time!'

The house is characterised by bespoke furniture, vintage pieces and a whimsical sense of design. The couple loves objects with a story and history. 'The old carpet in the hall once belonged to my grandmother. An old chest that was owned by my father and his father before him is now a place to store dressing-up clothes for the children. I also adore the old chairs we found for the kids in France, as well as the vintage school desk in the playroom. But I also love new handmade furniture produced by small businesses that create their pieces with love. All the other new furniture we bought is easy to replace. I'm not very attached to it,' says Tessa.

But the most important thing is a house that's a fun place to live in, that kids can play in as much as they like. Tessa: 'We designed the house to be an enjoyable home for all five of us. The boys can play, run, skate and even swing without a care. Our furniture is pretty sturdy. Our only rule is no one's allowed to eat on the HAY sofa. We wanted to create an environment where our boys can play, live and be themselves. And if that means they draw on the walls now and then, that's okay...'

Anyone who invites the Live Loud Girl interior team to create a design for a children's room can expect a daring colour combination with a beautiful timeless base. Simple, yet exceptional, it's a space that's full of surprises.

tropical touch for twins

residents

Sarah (caterer) and Liam
(estate agent) with twin daughters
Lina and Mila (7 months)
Dubai
Want to see more?
@liveloudgirl of liveloudgirl.com

The showstopper in this room is undoubtedly the Bien Fait wallpaper. It creates an instant wow effect, and even when they're older, the girls will love it. Because nurseries deserve a splash of colour, a bright yellow wall rack was added together with two Muuto wall hooks for a fun contrast against the black-and-white wallpaper.

In place of a classic changing table, an unused dining table was given a new lease of life by being given a gorgeous pink blush shade, and the bedside tables were painted to match. When the twins have outgrown nappies, the large table can get a makeover and serve a new function, so it's here to stay. Linda from Live Loud Girl is a big fan of furniture that will last for years and that can always be revamped to play a different role in the interior.

You know this is a cute twins' room by the identical Oeuf NYC beds, but the mismatching Konges Sløjd cloud mobiles and the blue-and-pink chair made from recycled plastic by Ecobirdy in Belgium make the space unique to each girl. A dreamy room with a twist of individuality for these lovely twins!

With plans to start a family, Ben and Line searched for a house with several bedrooms and a nice garden. Shortly after completing the purchase, Line discovered she was pregnant. Luckily, they hadn't planned any major renovations. The couple put their own individual stamp on their charming townhouse with paint, wallpaper and a new kitchen. And all in time to welcome the baby.

residents
Line (visual merchandiser),
Ben (product designer)
and daughter Lou (18 months)
Antwerp, Belgium
Want to see more?
@line_vanvoorden

little oasis
for mini
plant lady

Line was given carte blanche to furnish the nursery, but discussed the decor of all the other rooms with Ben. 'I wanted Lou's room to radiate joy, and it's certainly a space that makes you happy. Her room makes you smile. And, just as I did in all the other rooms, colour and plants are part of the decor. There was also lots of scope for adding new, playful twists: animals and children's books,' she explains.

Line picked a wallpaper by Roomblush as the base for Lou's room, and continued the green - and - pink colour scheme. While she was pregnant, Line was often unable to sleep at night and surfed second-hand sites, where she discovered the pink wardrobe and the vintage rocking swan, which happens to be identical to the one Line had as a child.

One of Line's favourite elements in the room is Lou's birth announcement card that she had printed in poster size. It adds a personal touch. And there's no coincidence that the colours are the exact shades chosen for the room.

Lou doesn't just sleep in her room – it's somewhere she often enjoys playing and reading. The room is bathed in lovely natural light during the day, so it would be a shame not to enjoy it.

Unfortunately, there was no room for a playroom – for that, the house would need an extra floor – but a tepee for Lou was set up in the living room, with storage boxes for the toys behind it. Lou also has her own little corner of the kitchen, a mini version of the 'real' kitchen. 'Lou has little play areas all over the house. And we hope she'll soon learn to clear up after herself, because we're doing that for her at the moment,' laughs Line.

Stylish living with children starts here!

ONLINE

An uber-luxurious online shop with accessories nurseries and children's rooms. If you don't find it here, you won't find it anywhere: **lidor.nl**

Antiques and vintage for big and small: **yapstock.com**

Beds and bedding for the smallest and almost adult children: **littledreamers.nl**

Customised bedding, wallpaper and bespoke advice on styling children's rooms: **bibelotte.nl**

Bespoke minimalist furnishings for the nursery. All items are made to order only: **woodchuck.nl**

Family concept store with a huge selection and irresistible items. Plus a fantastic 'outlet' section: **smallable.com**

Online shop with a mix of big famous brands, small French designers and handmade items for unique children's rooms: **lejoli-shop.com**

Posters, postcards and beautiful board games from Scandinavia: **vissevasse.com**

Betón has grown from a mini-collection of handmade leather children's slippers into a fully fledged children's store brimming with (living) accessories: **betonstudios.com**

Ecological, sustainable and affordable children's furniture: **muebleslufe.com**

Beautiful posters for the nursery, with a new exclusive and unique selection every season: **madomado.com**

The creative kids' stuff you buy here will last for generations to come: **olivelovesalfie.co.uk**

Original, playful and affordable wallpaper: **papermint.fr**

Rugs that are machine washable? Look no further! You'll find a wonderful selection here: **lorenacanals.com**

Each plush toy was handcrafted by second-generation teddy bear maker Jen Murphy: **polkadotclub.com**

For the biggest selection of rattan furniture and toys: **poppyslittletreasures.com**

Carpets, rocking chairs, cushions, storage baskets and much more: **hunterandnomad.com**

The most beautiful things from all over the world for parents with a passion for design: **littlegatherer.com**

Baby items that are inspired by all things high quality, gorgeous and practical: **peppapenny.com**

Handmade doll furniture and other fun wooden toys: **tinyharlow.com**

Educational toys, timeless children's clothing and decorative gadgets for the playroom and children's bedroom: **monkeynmoo.myshopify.com**

If you're looking for something to inspire and stimulate your children, check out the wide range of wooden and felt toys and educational materials at: **themallfolk.com**

The families featured in this book shop here.

A paradise for kids and their parents thanks to the unique range of decoration and furniture and the diverse clothing collections for children up to 12 years old: **rewinddesign.be**

One of the largest children's stores in Belgium, with a wide selection of toys, home accessories and clothing. A fairy-tale shop for young and old: **hetlandvanooit.be**

A stunning selection of mostly Nordic timeless brands. Having a baby doesn't mean everything has to be pink or blue! Discover the exceptional at: **hyggekids.be**

Everything for babies and children, with an eye for design, functionality, colour and sustainable materials. Discover wonderful things you'll happily welcome into your home at: **room4kids.be**

A selection of contemporary items and vintage finds. Timeless items to transform your home into a magical place: **archive-store.nl**

After the hugely successful selection of bedlinens for adults, check out the amazing selection of bedding for kids of all ages. You can match! **crispsheets.com**

Natural sheepskin items for your home and stroller, hand produced by one of the last remaining British tanneries. They keep your kids warm in winter and cool during hot summer days: **binibamba.com**

All the wooden toys and decorative attributes are carefully designed and selected to guarantee an original product. As they have a great selection of books, too: **moonpicnic.com**

Decorative elements is what this shop is all about. Think: wallpapers, bedding, lighting, prints and illustrations. Everything you need to create a unique children's room in any style: **theyoungsters.se**

Child-friendly home decor that will never go out of fashion and all chosen for functionality and design. You can find brands like OYOY Mini, Nofred and Meri Meri, and much more: **minifili.com**

This book is
MARKED

MARKED is an initiative by Lannoo Publishers.
markedbylannoo.com

Join the marked community on
⊙ | f @markedbylannoo

Or sign up for our MARKED newsletter with news about new and forthcoming publications on art, interior design, food & travel, photography and fashion as well as exclusive offers and MARKED events on www.markedbylannoo.com

Author
Joni Vandewalle

Editing and translation
Lisa Holden

Graphic design
De Poedelfabriek

If you have any questions or comments about the material in this book, please do not hesitate to contact our editorial team: markedteam@lannoo.com.

© Lannoo Publishers, Belgium, 2020
D/2020/45/405– NUR 454
ISBN: 9789401471374

www.lannoo.com

#AREYOUMARKED

Credits

Playful serenity
© Hannelore Veelaert

DIY dream room
© Anna Malmberg

Family house with history
© Penny Wincer

A messy house is a happy house
© Hannelore Veelaert

Year-round holiday home
© GAP Interiors/Julien Fernandez

Party of five
© Hannelore Veelaert

Tranquil but colourful
© Janniche Kristoffersen

Vintage girls' house
© Hannelore Veelaert

An explosion of colour and art
© Penny Wincer

Preloved is lovely
© Emma Sundh

Playing together under the eaves
© Hannelore Veelaert

From dark garage to light, open-plan house
© Jeltje Janmaat

House of cubs
© Isabel Macchia

Contemporary sixties vibes
© Hannelore Veelaert

Extraordinary living
© Hannelore Veelaert

Better together
© Hannelore Veelaert

Of rattan and rainbows
© Margaux Follis

XXL playhouse
© Hannelore Veelaert

Townhouse bursting with variety
© GAP Interiors/Julien Fernandez

Ever-changing
© Aylin Sleper

A nod to art nouveau
© GAP Interiors/Julien Fernandez

Dark but bright
© Sladjana Penjoc

A holiday mood
© Jeltje Janmaat

Tropical touch for twins
© Natelee Cocks Photography

Little oasis for mini plant lady
© Hannelore Veelaert